LIFE-SIZE

LIFE-SIZE

Poems by

J.R. Solonche

Cover design by Shay Culligan

ISBN: 978-1-63980-055-1

Kelsay Books
502 South 1040 East, A-119
American Fork, Utah 84003
Kelsaybooks.com

Books by J.R. Solonche

The Five Notebooks of Zhao Li

Selected Poems 2002-2021

Years Later

The Dust

A Guide of the Perplexed

For All I Know

The Moon Is the Capital of the World

Piano Music

Enjoy Yourself

The Time of Your Life

The Porch Poems

To Say the Least

A Public Place

True Enough

If You Should See Me Walking on the Road

I, Emily Dickinson and Other Found Poems

Tomorrow, Today and Yesterday

In Short Order

Invisible

Heart's Content

Won't Be Long

Beautiful Day

Acknowledgments

The Buddhist Poetry Review: "Dandelions," "How Nice,"
  "Life-Size"

The Daily Drunk: "Ice"

Hole in the Head Review: "Circle Square"

London Grip: "To Tim"

Contents

Life-Size

Nature abhors a panorama.
The snowflake is in the cherry blossom.

The gnat is in the eagle's wing.
Make yourself small.

Then make yourself smaller.
Then make yourself life-size.

Gravity

Graves are not exempt
even though they're
in the family.

Consciousness

Let them get off on it,
the philosophers, the physicists.

Let them get it on,
the Buddhists. the neuroscientists.

All I need to know is how to turn it off.
And turn it on again.

Improvements

I could make them if I chose to.
I could add this.
I could subtract that.
I could change this color.
I could change that shape.
Or I could leave well enough alone,
which is how well enough has always been left.

Wind Chimes

The chimes
are still
and silent
until
the wind
chimes in.

Very Short Conversation at the Bar

"Are you holding the door
for me?" I asked.
"Yes, but I won't hold
it forever," she answered.
"Why not? I would hold it
forever for you," I said.
That's as far as it got.

Waitless

Waiting for the hummingbirds
to arrive from there
is a weightless wait,
for the mind turns on its own wings
that weigh nothing,
nothing but air.

Corrections

There are so many,
you say you wouldn't
know where to begin.
But you would know
that in order to obviate
all the others to come,
it would have to be at
the beginning. Oh, if you
only knew when that was,
if you only knew where that
was, if you only knew that one.

Eva

My neighbor, Eva, just turned ninety-seven.
You'll be a hundred before you know it, I said.
No, I won't.
This was my last birthday, she said.
No, you still have three to go, I said.
I hope not.
I've had enough.
I wish this were Oregon, she said.
Why's that? I said.
Then I could get assisted suicide, she said.
Well, you could simply stop eating, I said.
No, I like food too much, she said.
Do you know the story of Diogenes? I said.
Who's that?
Does he live in Oregon? she said.
No, he lived in ancient Greece.
He was a philosopher, I said.
So? she said.
So it is said he died by refusing to breathe, I said.
Good trick.
But I couldn't, she said.
I couldn't either.
It's a story.
Who knows if it's true? I said.
I think it's true, she said and dozed off.

Fence Deference

Although the rails
have fallen and only
the posts are in the ground,
four stand-ins for a fence
no longer recognizable,
I'll leave them alone,
for this morning I saw
a goldfinch perched atop one,
flickering like a flame in the wind.

Radiant Connections

Ammons, these afternoons,
when the shadows lengthen
and widen, the sun still makes
its slender connections
that reach to brush
the cheeks of the trees
on the far end of the lawn.

Country Cemetery

Nameless blanks with no
need for the surface,
the stones, too, will follow
them down below
ground soon enough,
to leave up here only
the gravestones' graves.

Zenish

As long as it
never becomes
total selflessness,
I'm just fine
with the less
self the better.

Hopelessness Is a Thing with Feathers

An ostrich
has feathers
but cannot fly.
Do you think
it knows why?

April

Chaucer knew it
centuries
before Eliot,
this month at
the root of cruelty.

How Nice

How nice it is to sit
outside on a warm,
sunny, bright day
and not give the world
a second thought.
Or even a first thought.

Nietzsche

Nietzsche had it right
about remembering
your whip when you go
to woman. Bring it
quickly, though, before
she brings it to you.

Sound

Each thing sounds
the sound of itself.

The bird behind me
sounds its bird sound.

The plane above me
sounds its plane sound.

The chainsaw next to me
sounds its saw sound.

All around,
cacophony sounds.

Time

It doesn't matter
if it exists or not.
We barely have
enough of it
to know what it is.
Still, I hope it doesn't.

Bathless Birdbath

When the weather
warms up, I will fill it,
but for now how
forlorn it looks,
the birdbath without
the water for the birds' bath.

Redundant

"The rocket with the astronauts
took off in upward ascent,"
wrote the student. I didn't
correct it. I liked it, for I saw
it meant successful liftoff
as opposed to the failure
of a downward ascent.
I liked it.

Esmeralda

I, too, was in love with her.
Who wasn't?
Maureen O'Hara,
who wasn't in love with you?
We all were.
But I wouldn't have been the captain.
I would have been
the hunchback, high, high above,
ringing and singing and ringing
and singing the bells
of love for her.
O, I would have been
Quasimodo,
singing and ringing the bells high above for her,
for Esmeralda,
for O'Hara.

Dandelions

Now that the dandelions
have gone to seed,
have become all gray-headed overnight,
they wait for just the right wind
to scatter them anyplace all over the place.

Spoiler

It's always there.
Just out of sight.
Just around the corner.
Just down the road.
Just coming out the back.
The spoiler.
The soiler.
The foiler.
You know who I mean.
You've seen him many times.
The same slicked back hair.
The same weasely little eyes.
The same big fat mouth.

Full

The woods are full of green.
The sky is full of blue.
Both are full of gold.
So why is the world,
this world of women,
this world of men,
so why is the world so full of shit?

The Fool of Green

Have you met
The Fool of Green?
Have you seen
The Fool of Gold?

One is young
And lean.
One is fat
And old.

Have you seen
The Fool of Gold?
Have you met
The Fool of Green?

One is not as bad
As he seems.
One is not as good
As is told.

Perennials

It's not so much
that they return
every year as that
there are more of
them every year.
The best part is
underground.

On My Behalf

Say of him:
"He never meant any harm."

Say of him:
"He always meant harmless."

Say of him:
"We shall never think him charmless."

Library

I'm not in the library.
I'm thinking about the library.
The library is one of my favorite places not to be.
The other is the synagogue, church of the Hebrews.
I do go to the library.
I go there to take out books.
But I don't stay there.
I don't sit in the reading room.
I don't sit outside on a bench.
I get the book and leave.
I think it's because the library is so intimidating.
It's full of books from floor to ceiling that I'll never read.
And the librarians remind me of my fourth grade teacher.
They all do.
Her name was Mrs. Pogrow who exhorted me to read.
I don't like the synagogue for the same reasons.
It's so intimidating.
There's the Five Books of Moses behind the purple velvet curtain.
There's the rabbi up there looking down.
He reminds me of my tenth grade English teacher who exhorted
me to study.
Here I am surrounded by the old men.
They point their beards at me like accusing fingers.
There is one thing to say in the synagogue's favor.
There are only five books I'll never read.

Privacy

The big red-headed
woodpecker sees me
and flies off. I completely
understand his need
for privacy. It's my tree.

Cacophony

It was all the birds
all the time until
my neighbor's log
splitter kicked in
and kicked them out.

Swan Swamp

The swan pair
has moved from
the lake to the swamp
where the water is calmer,
which is too bad,
for now no one
will be able to write
a ballet about them.

English Ivy

If it weren't for
the eight-foot deer
fence, where would
the English Ivy be?
Not around here.

Crimson Azalea

So red, so red,
what is its terrible
secret for it to be
so embarrassed
for so long?

Breakthrough

Above the gray
clouds, the blue
sky breaks through
just enough to let
the sun through
before it's through.

Circle Square

The town square in
my town is called *Circle
Square*. There's a church.
There's a library. There
are two bars. I went
into the library to find
out how it got its name.
They told me it was
named by the town's
founder who was a math
teacher with a sense
of humor. I went into
the church and asked
the pastor how it got
its name. He said that
the town's first pastor
named it for the greater
glory of God for whom
nothing is impossible.
I went into the first bar.
They said it was named
for the town's first drunk
who stumbled in circles
around the square until
he fell flat on his face.
I went into the second
bar. They told me the same
story. Makes sense to me.

The Sky Was Busy Today

The sky was busy today.
There were five planes.
There were eight birds.
There were twelve clouds.
I was busy counting the twenty-five skies today.

The Earth Says

The earth says, Have a place.
The earth says, I have many.
The earth says, I have more than enough for all of you.
The earth says, But listen carefully.
The earth says, Do not call it your own.
The earth says, Especially your final resting place.
That especially do not call your own, the earth says.

Home

In the early morning, when
the sun is still a tree
and the tree is still mythology
and mythology is still the dream
that refuses to go away quietly,
I am home.

Peony Buds

If you hadn't seen them before,
you would not know
what these peony buds have in store.
Their heads will be the heft of cabbages.
Their color will be as rich roses,
and they will be weighed
down as though from the color alone.
If left on their own,
they will bow so low
to the ground they will look like
they are bowing before a king
who will never tell them to arise and go.

Forgiveness

I went to the Rushing Duck Brewery the first time in a year.
I ordered a beer, *Divided by Zero*.
I didn't recognize the barmaid.
I thought she must have been new.
Put on your mask, Joel, she said.
How do you know my name? I asked.
I know you, she said.
You've been coming here for years, she said.
I recognized her.
It was Loretta.
Loretta, I'm so sorry, I said.
I didn't recognize you, I said.
It must be the mask, I said.
That's all right, she said.
It's been a long time, she said.
I forgive you, she said.
No, there's no excuse, I said.
Please do not forgive me, I said.
You don't want me to forgive you? she asked.
No, never ever forgive me, I said.
But why? she asked.
Because I want to know how it feels to be unforgiven, I said.
To be unforgiven for something for the rest of my life, I said.
Sorry, Joel, but I forgive you, she said.
You'll have to find somebody else to not forgive you, she said.
All right, Loretta, you win, I said.
I will, I said.
If it's the last thing I do, I said.
But I hope the one who will never forgive is as beautiful as you, I
said.

Monday

My neighbor has a garden.
Someday I want to ask him
if he knows what Voltaire
said about tending gardens,
but I won't. Yesterday, I saw
him and his wife and his kids
dressed in their Sunday best.

Fame

This morning I heard
that Gorman kid
read on the radio.
She was—I don't know—
so melodramatic
that she sounded sick,
gasping, out of breath,
reading the damn thing to death.
Fame has gotten to her head,
all right. Poor kid. Poor kid.

Shine!

Shine clouds!
Shine trees!

Shine grass!
Shine peonies!

Shine crows!
Shine in the sunshine

that does not need
our exhortation.

Again and Time

Again alone and with time
on one's hands and
with hands on one's time,
I make the most
of my time whatever the cost,
for there's no making up for the lost.

This Place

The future will
happen here
or not at all.

Day

It includes night
when used that way,
but is half itself
when lengthened to daylight.

For Samuel Menashe

What took you years took me
an hour. Therefore we must agree
that time does not exist,
or that it does—with a devilish twist.

Footfall

I hear you behind me,
your signature tick-
tock signal of time,
your unmistakable
foot falling.

Pastoral

Once it was the test
of a poet's skill,
the first piece published,
written well past oral.

Lust

It drives desire mad
like the whip does horses.
It drives the grasses
and all green things
mad for the sun.
It drives men and women
wild for each other.
There is no other word
for it except, *Must!*

Religion

It was not a difficult decision
to leave my religion.
Yahweh
made it easy
by doing things his way.

Neglect

Does the garden know
it is neglected?
I can't imagine so.
Just see how the weeds stand proud.
Not so far.
Just hear how loud
the crickets are.

The Last Words of My Mother

Whatever you do is fine, she said.
I did nothing.
I left her bedside.
I left her room.
I left the hospital.
I answered the phone two days later.
I said, Thank you.
I went to the cemetery.
I buried her next to her husband.
I said to my cousins, I will.
I never did.
They knew I never would.
Did they know whatever I did was fine?
I did nothing.
It was fine.

Dementia

They are there,
those who are not there.
The father is there who is not there.
The mother is there who is not there.
The aunt is there who is not there.
The uncle is there who is not there.
The doctor is there who is not there.
The friends are there who are not there.
Her heaven is their hell.
One day one is there.
One day the other.

Ashes

In place of fire
in the fireplace,
where heat at hearth's heart was,
colder than memory,
ashes are.

Idol

Of course it was a calf
of gold. What else could it
have been but the very animal
Yahweh demands as sacrifice
to him? But gold does not bleed
as the real red heifer does
on the temple's altar, the blood
which is his and his alone.

Inheritance

Someday you'll be rich,
she said. She said that
more than once, so
I believed it. I'm glad
it wasn't true. I'm not
good with money.
I bought a Honda C-RV
and gave the rest to charity.

Prayer

Give us our daily bread
by which man does not live alone.

Ruins

Stones first come
to mind. Then wood.
Then iron. Then glass.
Then finally the mind
which no longer knows
the place of glass, of iron,
of wood, of stone,
comes to mind.

Paradise

Paradise is motionlessness.
The momentous moment
between movements.
The meeting of eyes.
The blink of an eye everlasting.
This is paradise.
I know this.
I have seen it with my own eyes.

Spirea

One must get close,
very close, to hear
them speak their shy
white words under
their breath above
your breath.

Peony Petals

The peonies fall
apart, their petals
superfluous now,
their wondrous work done
for the next generation
to pick up their part.

Luna Moth

I tried to help it turn
over, but it seemed not
to want to, for
every time I got
it on its feet, it flipped
back over again.
It's gone now,
cursing me under
its Luna moth breath,
no doubt.

The Sonnet of Answers

Yes, I did search for another star.
No, it wasn't home that night.
Yes, I left a note right on the door.
No, there was no porch light.

No, I could not read the words.
Yes, she looked sideways but not around.
No, I'm sure that they were only birds.
Yes, she put that on. It was that sound.

Yes, it was the window with the sun.
No, I don't remember that I slept.
Yes, I swear she was the only one.
No, I don't remember that I wept.

No, I didn't go. I didn't go.
Yes, I was a fool. I know. I know.

War

Perhaps it does make sense.
Perhaps it is a necessity,
it's been around so long, at
least as long as we have been.
I think we won't be really
human until the day it's gone
forever. But then we'll
have to find another name
for who we are just to make
sure it's out of our system
for good. *Angels,* maybe.
Or *hippies.* Or *houyhnhnms.*
Yes, *houyhnhnms,* definitely.

Ice

I honor how
they sacrifice
themselves, these
cubes of ice in
my Irish whiskey.
"We'll be free
and won't be back,"
is the stupid joke
I hear them crack.

History

When did it begin?
Did it begin this morning?
Did it begin yesterday?
Did it begin last week?
Did it begin last month?
Did it begin last year?
Did it begin
when the historian
says it does?
When *Is* is *Was?*

Shred of Cloud

What is it doing there,
that shred of cloud
in the middle of blue?
Ah, never mind.
There is goes, evaporated.

Summer in Sumer

It was hot there
in Sumer
in summer.
Nevertheless,
the first poet
wrote the first poem,
"Life is short.
Let us spend."

Shout

Why am I
the only one
not shouting
out loud among
all the shouters
on this sunny
afternoon? Oh,
but I am, I am.
Cover your ears
with your hands,
and you'll hear
me shouting louder
than all the others
put together.

White Peonies

So colorless,
what bee will come to it?
Surrounded by such sisters
magenta and pink,
what wasp will come to it?
Yet they come,
the bees, the wasps come to the white peonies.

Song of Loss

I've lost what teachers said.
I've lost my place in line.
I've lost trees, oak and pine.
But I've never lost my head.

I've lost a poem's thread.
I lost the blonde one, Joyce.
And Sue, my second choice.
But I've never lost my head.

I lost my best friend, Ted.
I lost one more to crime.
I've lost, oh, so much time.
But I've never lost my head.

Of snakes I lost my dread.
Of spiders lost my fear.
I've lost my fishing gear.
But I've never lost my head.

I've lost from A to Zed.
I've lost my shirt, the white.
I've lost my best eyesight.
But I've never lost my head.

Ammons, Did

Ammons, did
you hear?
"Charming weather,
reports," is how
they described
your poetry.
Shall I tell
them that a charm
is a spell?
No?
I didn't think
you would. I'll
let it go.

Around Here

It depends on
the day of the week.
It depends on
the hour of the day.
Usually quiet one way
or another.
But when the kids
get off their buses
and onto their dirt bikes,
and the fathers of the sons
spend their Saturdays
and Sundays on
their Harley-Davidsons,
I swear I don' know
how the birds know
where to go.

The Freight

What a horn
of mournful
warning it sounds
as it nears
the crossing as
though it has
already killed you.

It

What do
we need
to make of it
to make
of it?

Failure Story

There's nothing wrong
with a happy
beginning as long
as it ends there.

Old Frame

I found an old
gold-colored frame
without a picture,
only the glass
and the backing
board, but I hung it
above my desk
where it's just as
incompletely finished
as anyone.

Almost Counts

My friend, Jeff, is
hard of hearing, deaf,
I guess. It's hard to talk
to him. He's constantly
fiddling with his hearing
aids and making faces.
Nevertheless, conversations
are quite interesting.
They're almost poems.

Shower

I hate to watch
them go down
the drain,
the old skin cells,
the old sins,
leaving me no choice
but to grow new ones.

Boulder

Alone on the grass
at the edge
of the lawn where
the split-rail fence
has fallen,
how magnanimous
it is to allow
the weeds to grow up
around it so tall.

Stardom

I saw a movie
called *Sound of Metal*
about a drummer
who plays rock music
so loud, he goes deaf.
I want to star in a movie
about a poet who
writes poems so loud
he, too, goes deaf.
I'll call it *Sound of Paper.*

Daisy

Dayseye, he called you best.
But what do you do, *dayseye,*
when you've seen enough?
How do you shut out the world,
and what do you do at night,
in the starry dark, when you must
outstare the moon, when you must
watch as she slides into the bliss of rest?

These Days

I asked the barmaid
if she read the book
I left at the bar last
month. I did, she said.
In fact, I took it home,
she said. In fact, after
I read "Masturbation,"
I put it under my pillow
and masturbated, she said.
You mean the poem
that goes, "Sorry, I got
ahead of myself?" I said.
Yeah, that's the one.
It made me horny, she
said. Thank you, I said
and finished my beer.
I left a twenty-dollar tip.

To Tim

I would have written *Dear Tim,*
but I reserve that word for the woman,
you know the woman I mean,
the one that once I call that word
I will call by that word exclusively,
so, Tim, thanks for your letter,
I'm unable to be casual about it,
about that word *dear,* probably
because I'm a poet but more likely
because I'm a damned fool, so
anyway thanks for your kind letter,
I haven't found her yet, the woman
for whom I'm saving *dear,* I'm
sure I never will, I'm seventy-four,
cool photo of you playing the guitar,
I'd give a hundred poems to be able
to play an instrument, don't get
me wrong, I've known my share
of women, but none measured up to
the ideal woman we all discover in
our heads at puberty and then carry
around in there for the rest of our lives,
to answer your question, I'm doing it
now, sitting outside in what remains of
daylight, drinking what remains of Jim
Beam, writing this, I don't know how
the *Dear* salutation started, do you?
I should look it up, I do it every day,
preferably outdoors, but everyday
is the main thing, do you have a word
that you simply refuse to use in a poem?
send me a poem using the word you hold
most sacred, that you value most dearly,

that you have sworn never to use, I looked
it up, according to the *Online Etymological
Dictionary,* "As a polite introductory
word to letters, it is attested from mid-15c.
The military man's dreaded *Dear John
letter* is attested from 1945. As a noun,
from late 14c., perhaps short for dear one."

Best,

Alan Dugan

I once wrote a poem about him.
No, it was a poem about his death,
which is the same thing, I suppose
as a poem about him. I want to write
another one, but I don't know what
to say that I didn't say the first time.
Let's just say that I might be the only
poet who actually reads his poetry.
Let's just say that the same people
who ignore Alan Dugan ignore me.

After a Reading

A woman came up to me.
She was the pianist
of the Radio City
Music Hall orchestra.
"You're a composer.
It's all music," she said.
Finally.

About the Author

Nominated for the National Book Award and twice-nominated for the Pulitzer Prize, J.R. Solonche is the author of twenty-six books of poetry and coauthor of another. He lives in the Hudson Valley.

Made in the USA
Middletown, DE
22 December 2021